Robert E. Lee

Candice Ransom

LERNER PUBLICATIONS COMPANY • MINNEAPOLIS

In memory of Willard F. Figley, another true gentleman

Illustrations by Tim Parlin

Lerner Publications Company
A division of Lerner Publishing Group
241 First Avenue North
Minneapolis, MN 55401 U.S.A.

Website address: www.lernerbooks.com

Library of Congress Cataloging-in-Publication Data

Ransom, Candice F., 1952–
    Robert E. Lee / by Candice Ransom.
      p.   cm. — (History maker bios)
    Includes bibliographical references and index.
    ISBN: 0–8225–2437–6 (lib. bdg. : alk. paper)
    1. Lee, Robert E. (Robert Edward), 1807–1870—Juvenile literature. 2. Generals—Confederate States of America—Biography—Juvenile literature. 3. Confederate States of America. Army—Biography—Juvenile literature. I. Title. II. Series.
E467.1.L4R35 2005
973.7'3'092—dc22   2004019506

Manufactured in the United States of America
1 2 3 4 5 6 – JR – 10 09 08 07 06 05

TABLE OF CONTENTS

INTRODUCTION

Robert E. Lee has been called the greatest soldier of the American Civil War. The silver-haired man in the gray coat on the gray horse became a symbol of the Confederate South.

Robert was born to be a soldier. He was intelligent, strong, and hardworking. He believed that serving his country was a noble job. But he never wanted to fight other Americans.

After the war, Robert put down his sword and did his best to heal the nation. Robert E. Lee may have been the United States' most beloved general.

This is his story.

1 A GOOD SON

Robert Edward Lee was born on January 19, 1807, in Westmoreland County, Virginia. His family lived in Stratford Hall, a mansion overlooking the Potomac River.

The Lees were an important family in Virginia. Robert's father was Henry "Light-Horse Harry" Lee, a hero of the American Revolution. His mother, Ann Carter Lee, came from a wealthy family. Two of Robert's relatives signed the Declaration of Independence.

But Robert's family was not rich. Life at Stratford Hall was hard for Robert, his two brothers, and his sister. The family lived in only a few rooms of the huge house. They could not afford to heat the whole house.

Robert's father, Henry Lee, was a hero in the American Revolution.

Stratford Hall had been a large, successful tobacco farm, called a plantation. But Robert's father spent the family's money on bad business deals. Henry then sold land, horses, and furniture to pay the bills. What Henry did not sell, sheriffs took away. In 1809, Henry went to jail for not paying his debts.

When Henry got out of jail a year later, he moved the family to Alexandria, Virginia. Alexandria was a bustling port across the Potomac River from Washington, D.C. The Lees settled in a small house. Soon a baby girl joined the family.

A WEALTH OF COUSINS

Robert was shy with strangers. But he was always comfortable with relatives. Both the Lees and the Carters had very large families. Robert had many cousins in Alexandria and throughout Virginia. The cousins swam in the Potomac River and played on the hillsides of family estates. One of Robert's closest friends was his cousin Cassius Lee.

Robert was born at Stratford Hall in Virginia.

Henry did not stay with the family long. He had health problems and wanted to live in a warmer climate. In 1813, he sailed to the West Indies, islands in the Caribbean Sea. Robert was six. He never saw his father again.

Robert's mother was also in poor health. The family lived on a small amount of money she had. It was not quite enough. Often Robert and his brothers had to share one piece of chicken for supper.

In 1818, Robert's brother Carter moved to New York City. His brother Smith joined the navy. Only Robert was left to care for his sickly mother and his sisters.

At thirteen, Robert entered the Alexandria Academy, a local school. He continued to take care of the household and nurse his mother. On many afternoons, he took his mother for carriage rides. When the weather was cold, he would stuff paper in the cracks of their run-down carriage to keep the cold wind out.

Strangers may have thought Robert was unfriendly. But he was really very shy and serious. He felt responsible for his mother and sisters. Robert did not want to be like his father. He did not want to disappoint people who depended on him.

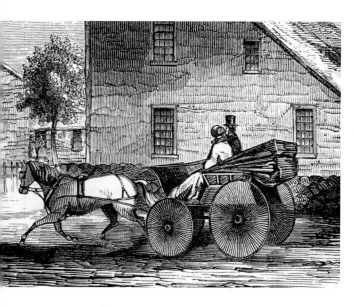

The Lee family's carriage may have looked like this one.

After finishing school, Robert knew he couldn't afford college. But the U.S. Military Academy at West Point, New York, offered a free education. Robert knew that after West Point, he could earn a living as a soldier. In 1825, he left for West Point.

At West Point, life was tough for the students, who were called cadets. West Point had many rules to teach cadets order and obedience. When they were not in class, cadets had to study or practice military training.

Lee was used to working hard. The rules did not bother him. He got up at 5:30 every morning. He marched, studied, and attended classes until four in the afternoon. He ate boiled meat and potatoes for nearly every meal.

Robert wore a uniform like this one as a cadet at West Point.

Lee wanted to be the perfect cadet. He kept his uniform spotless and his shoes polished. He was never late to class. In four years, he never earned a single bad mark for breaking a rule.

Lee graduated from West Point in 1829. He was the second best student in his class for grades and discipline. He joined the Army Corps of Engineers. As a member of the corps, Lee would design army forts and bridges. He looked forward to his career.

Young Lee was a handsome soldier.

2 THE BEST SOLDIER

After graduation, Lee went to live with his mother in Washington, D.C. But his mother was very sick and died that summer. Lee took comfort in being near one of his childhood friends, Mary Custis. She lived at Arlington House, across the Potomac from Washington.

Lee continued to call on Mary through the next year. Lee was handsome, with a straight nose, wavy black hair, and brown eyes. Mary was smart, pretty, and lively. The couple fell in love. In June 1831, they were married at Arlington House.

THE WASHINGTON CONNECTION

Lee's father, Henry, had been one of General George Washington's officers during the American Revolution. Henry remained friends with Washington after he became the first president of the United States. But Mary Custis Lee had an even closer connection to the father of the country. George Washington was the second husband of Martha Custis Washington, Mary's great-grandmother. Mary's father was Martha's grandson. Martha and George raised him after his parents died.

While Mary stayed at Arlington House, Lee began traveling for his military career. He moved up the ranks quickly. In 1838, he was promoted to captain of the engineers.

Lee and Mary had seven children during this time: George, Mary, William, Annie, Agnes, Robert Jr., and Millie. Though Lee was often away, he wanted his children to feel loved. He told them stories, taught them to ride horses, and brought them pets. Lee also wanted to pass on a sense of duty. The children had to do chores and obey their parents.

Lee continued to work hard at his career. He had been a soldier for years but had never seen a battle. The United States had been at peace for a long time.

But that peace was broken when the United States declared war on Mexico on May 13, 1846. The U.S. and Mexican governments were fighting over the southern border of Texas.

Lee was sent to Mexico with the army. During the Mexican-American War, he learned how awful war could be. But he did his duty as a soldier. For his bravery, he was made a colonel. U.S. Army general Winfield Scott called Lee "the very best soldier I have seen in the field."

The Battle of Churubusco (BELOW) in the Mexican-American War gave Lee a chance to prove himself.

In 1855, Lee joined the cavalry (soldiers who fight on horseback) in Texas. During this time, another fight was beginning. But this time, the fight was not with another country. Northern and Southern states were arguing with each other.

For many years, the North and the South had been divided over slavery. Southerners used African American slaves to work on plantations. But slavery was against the law in the North. Some Northerners wanted slavery to be illegal in every state in the United States, which was called the Union.

Many African American slaves worked on cotton plantations.

In 1860, an antislavery president, Abraham Lincoln, was elected. Southerners were afraid Lincoln would end slavery in the South. The Southerners felt the North had no right to tell them what to do. Beginning in December 1860, seven Southern states broke away from the Union. They formed a new government, the Confederate States of America. They elected Jefferson Davis as their president.

On April 12, 1861, Confederate soldiers attacked the Union army at Fort Sumter in South Carolina. After the battle at Fort Sumter, four more states, including Virginia, joined the Confederacy. The Civil War had begun.

The Civil War started at Fort Sumter.

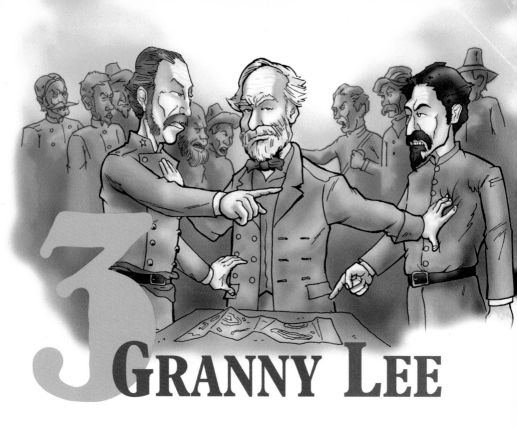

3 GRANNY LEE

Lincoln did not believe that states had
a right to break away from the Union.
He believed that the Confederate rebellion
must be stopped. Union soldiers would
have to take over rebel states and force the
Confederate government to surrender.

Lincoln asked Lee to head the Union
army. Lee was torn. He was loyal to
the United States, and he disagreed
with slavery.

But Lee was also a Virginian. He could not lead an army against his home state. Lee felt he had no choice. He quit the U.S. Army and returned to Arlington.

Soon after, Virginia governor John Letcher asked him to come to Richmond. Richmond was Virginia's state capital and the capital of the new Confederacy. Letcher wanted Lee to command Virginia's military. Lee agreed. He began choosing his officers. He chose men such as Thomas Jackson and James Ewell Brown "Jeb" Stuart.

Under Lee's command, the officers took charge of parts of Virginia's army. Lee stayed in Richmond to work on war plans with President Davis.

Lee (FAR RIGHT) and Confederate president Davis (SEATED) relied on Jeb Stuart (STANDING, SECOND FROM LEFT), Thomas Jackson (THIRD FROM LEFT), and other skilled officers.

LEAVING ARLINGTON HOUSE

As soon as the war began, Lee knew the Union army would take over Arlington House. He urged Mary to leave. At first, she refused. But in May 1861, she moved the family to Richmond. Union troops took over the Arlington estate and built forts there. The Union army later began using the grounds as a cemetery for soldiers killed in the war. It eventually became Arlington National Cemetery, still used by the U.S. Armed Forces.

Lee and Davis knew the Union planned to invade Richmond and capture Confederate leaders. Lee's army was ready. His officers led troops against the Union on July 21, 1861. The armies clashed outside a small Virginia town called Manassas Junction, near the Bull Run River.

The Confederates were outnumbered at the Battle of Bull Run. Yet they drove the Union forces away from Richmond. Lee's choice of officers had proven correct. Thomas Jackson saved the day. For holding back the Union forces, Jackson earned the nickname "Stonewall."

Back in Richmond, Lee continued to organize Virginia troops and work on war plans. But Lee wanted to be part of the action. In late summer 1861, Davis gave him his first battlefield command.

Lee (RIGHT) meets with Stonewall Jackson (LEFT) before a battle.

Union general George McClellan (SECOND FROM LEFT) welcomes U.S. president Lincoln to a Union camp.

General George McClellan's Union army had invaded western Virginia. Lee's job was to drive McClellan's troops out. But Lee spent most of his time trying to stop his officers from arguing with each other. Lee's first command was not a success, and he returned to Richmond.

Newspapers in Virginia covered Lee's failure to control his bickering officers. The newspapers compared him to a weak old woman. They called him "Granny Lee." But Davis had faith in Lee. In May 1862, Davis put Lee in charge of the largest Confederate force, the Army of Northern Virginia.

In the summer of 1862, Lee and McClellan's armies fought the Seven Days' Battles around Richmond. Confederate forces won the first six battles. But they lost the seventh on July 1. Lee's troops had to retreat. But the Union troops drew back too. Lee had saved Richmond from capture.

The Seven Days' Battles changed people's opinions of "Granny" Lee. Newspapers praised his skill. His officers and soldiers trusted Lee as a leader.

Confederate forces won the battle at Mechanicsville, Virginia. A newspaper reporter's sketch (BELOW) shows them leaving the city. Few Civil War reporters had cameras.

The Second Battle of Bull Run in Virginia was a Confederate victory too.

In August 1862, the armies clashed once more at Bull Run. Again, Lee's ability to plan battles and Jackson's ability to fight gave the Confederates another victory.

Lee was ready to make a daring move. He would not wait for the Union to attack the South. Instead, he would invade the North. If Lee could prove the Confederates were a strong fighting force, Northerners might lose faith in Lincoln's government.

In early September, Lee's thirty-five thousand soldiers crossed the Potomac River into Maryland. On September 17, they met McClellan's Union army of eighty-seven thousand in the Battle of Antietam.

Lee's smaller army fought hard. The battle ended at nightfall. The next day, McClellan did not attack. Lee's soldiers bravely stayed on the battlefield. But Lee knew they could not fight again. They had lost too many men and were out of food. He turned his army back across the Potomac. It was not a victory, but Lee's soldiers had fought well.

After the Union won the Battle of Antietam, Lincoln warned the Confederacy to stop fighting. He gave them until January 1, 1863, to stop fighting and return to the Union. If they refused, Lincoln said, all slaves in rebel states would be declared free. Lincoln's statement became the Emancipation Proclamation. Southerners were angry at the proclamation. It made them want to fight even harder against the Union.

4 THE GRAY FOX

As the Confederates considered new plans, Lee got bad news from home. His daughter Annie had died of a fever. But he could not go home to be with his family during this sad time. He had to keep fighting.

In November 1862, Union general Ambrose Burnside moved his army to the banks of the Rappahannock River in Virginia. Lee knew Burnside meant to cross the river and capture the town of Fredericksburg. Then Burnside would have an open road to Richmond, fifty miles away.

Lee hurried his army to the top of the hill behind Fredericksburg. From the hill, the Confederates easily fired on the Union soldiers with rifles and cannons.

The Confederates destroyed the bridge to Fredericksburg, Virginia, so that Union soldiers could not use it.

Lee sent riflemen into Fredericksburg to wait for Union soldiers to come into town.

Burnside ordered his troops to charge up the hill to fight Lee's troops. That was a bad mistake. Burnside's soldiers were left out in the open as the Confederates continued to fire on them.

Lee watched the battle through field glasses. By the end of the battle, thirteen thousand Union soldiers were dead or wounded on the field below the hill. Lee turned to one of his officers, James Longstreet. "It is well that war is so terrible—" he said, "we should grow too fond of it."

The victory at Fredericksburg made Lee a hero in the South. A soldier wrote to his family in Georgia, "We never can be whipped while we have such a leader as General Lee."

That winter, both armies rested. They did not fight again until May 1, 1863. Lee came up with a daring plan to divide his small army. One part of the army guarded Fredericksburg. The other, led by Jackson, attacked Union troops at Chancellorsville, Virginia. The battle raged for two days. Finally, the Union troops retreated. Once more, the Confederates had saved Richmond.

Lee rode his horse Traveller to the head of his army. Amid smoke and flames, his men cheered wildly. They called him the Gray Fox for his clever plan.

Some Union soldiers (BELOW CENTER) run from the tough battle at Chancellorsville.

TRAVELLER

As an army officer, Lee owned several horses over the years. But his favorite horse was Traveller. Traveller was born and raised in Virginia. His coat was Confederate gray. He was first offered to Lee as a gift. But Lee insisted on paying Traveller's owner a fair price. Lee rode Traveller into many Civil War battles. Traveller became almost as famous as Lee.

But the battle also brought a great loss for Lee and the Confederacy. Stonewall Jackson, Lee's best general, died after being wounded at Chancellorsville. "I know not how to replace him," Lee said sadly.

31

Lee decided to invade the North again. In late June 1863, his army marched into Pennsylvania. Lee's soldiers had seen only a few Union troops along the way. They had no idea that the huge Union Army of the Potomac was right behind them!

On July 1, Lee was forced to fight before he was ready, near the town of Gettysburg, Pennsylvania. Lee's army won the first battle, but the Union army held their ground outside the town. Lee ordered his troops to attack again on July 3. This time, the attack was a failure. Many Confederates were killed, and many others had to surrender.

This hill offers a good view of two roads to Gettysburg. Northern and Southern soldiers fought for control of it.

Gettysburg was a disaster for the Army of Northern Virginia. Lee felt it was all his fault. Late on the night of July 3, he rode Traveller back to his headquarters. One of his generals waited for him.

"Too bad!" the general heard Lee say. "Too bad! Oh, too bad!"

On July 5, Lee began to march his army back to Virginia. Lee wrote to Davis, offering to resign. Davis refused. The South needed Lee to help stop a serious threat— Union general Ulysses S. Grant.

Like Lee, Union general Ulysses S. Grant had a West Point education.

Lee was a feared military leader, but Grant (SECOND FROM RIGHT) was calm and sure of himself.

The Union army under Grant had been winning many battles in the West. They had taken control of the entire Mississippi River. Grant was now headed east to destroy the Army of Northern Virginia.

Grant planned to invade Virginia. Lee knew that Grant had to march his troops through the Wilderness, an area of thick woods and swamps. The Union's slow march through an unfamiliar place would give Lee an advantage in attacking. On May 5, 1864, the Battle of the Wilderness began.

The fighting continued for two days. Neither Grant nor Lee won the Battle of the Wilderness. But unlike the Union generals before him, Grant did not retreat. Lee knew Grant was a different enemy.

Grant kept his troops marching east. Lee kept his forces between Grant and Richmond. They fought in battle after battle. After each, Lee gave the signal to take down the tents and move on. "Strike the tent!" he commanded time and again.

Lee's fight to protect Richmond made him move his camp many times.

As the armies fought, Lee heard bad news from other parts of the South. Union troops led by William T. Sherman were burning homes and farms across Georgia. Union general Philip Sheridan was doing the same in Virginia's Shenandoah Valley. The Union wanted to destroy the South's will to fight.

Lee was the South's last hope. But Grant's army grew stronger and bigger every day. Lee came up with a plan. His army would slip away and join General Joseph Johnston's army in North Carolina. With more troops, Lee hoped to stop Sherman's army. Lee would then return to Virginia and take care of Grant.

Union troops pulled down telegraph wires and tore up railroad tracks in Georgia.

The people of Richmond, Virginia, flee as Grant's army sets the city on fire.

On April 2, 1865, the powerful Union army took over Richmond. Later, Lee heard that Richmond was in flames. He did not know that Mary and his family had escaped safely.

Lee urged his horse Traveller west. Grant's army was close behind Lee's men. Grant did not want Lee to reach Johnston's army. Grant caught up with Lee near the village of Appomattox Court House, Virginia. On April 9, 1865, more than 100,000 Union soldiers surrounded Lee's army. Lee had no choice but to surrender.

5 PRESIDENT LEE

On April 9, 1865, Lee put on his dress uniform and gold saber. He was to meet Grant at a house in Appomattox. If he was to be Grant's prisoner, he wanted to look like a proud soldier.

McLean House

Grant captured Lee's troops near the village of Appomattox Court House. The Wilmer McLean family lived in the village in a large redbrick house. On April 7, 1865, Lee and Grant met at the McLean home. The home became the site of the Confederate surrender. In the 1940s, Congress named Appomattox Court House a national landmark. McLean House was restored. In 1950, descendants of Robert E. Lee and U. S. Grant met at the house. They led a ceremony opening the historic home to the public.

Grant told Lee that Confederate soldiers would not be sent to prison. But they had to promise to go home to their farms and not fight again.

Lee asked Grant for food for his starving troops. Then he signed an agreement with Grant. The Confederacy had surrendered.

Lee walked slowly out onto the porch. He dreaded what he had to do next. He called for Traveller, swung wearily into the saddle, and rode one last time along his line of soldiers.

At first, his men cheered. Then they realized their leader had surrendered. They cried and patted Traveller. Tears filled Lee's eyes too. After four years, the war was over. Lee was going home to his family.

Lee's son George Washington Custis Lee (LEFT) and Walter Taylor, an officer on Lee's staff, stand beside Lee.

Lee rode Traveller home from Appomattox.

Many Southerners were bitter about the war. But Lee only wanted peace. Lee was still a hero in the South. He thought he could set an example. He urged people to put the war behind them and not hate the North. At social gatherings, he was often the first to talk to Northern visitors.

In August 1865, he was offered a job as president of Washington College in Lexington, Virginia. The college was poor, and its buildings were old. College leaders believed Lee would save the school. He accepted the job.

Working in this office, Lee made a lot of changes at Washington University.

As college president, Lee helped establish a law school. He encouraged the college to teach more science classes. And he began courses in business and journalism. They were the first business and news reporting classes ever offered in a U.S. college.

Each morning, Lee went to his office and found a basket full of letters from admirers. Each afternoon, he saddled Traveller for a long ride through Lexington. Along the way, people pulled hairs from Traveller's tail for souvenirs.

The college built a new president's house for Lee and Mary. But he only enjoyed it for sixteen months. On September 28, 1870, during dinner, Lee suffered a stroke.

Over the next several days, he slept deeply. But he seemed to dream of the war. On October 12, he awoke and gave his last order before dying: "Strike the tent."

For Lee's funeral on October 15, the college, Lexington, and Richmond were draped in black. Church bells tolled, and a military band played on muffled drums. Traveller walked behind the hearse.

Mary and Lee had never returned to Arlington House after the war. Washington College had become their home. After his death, Lee was buried beneath the college chapel. In time, Mary and the rest of the family were also laid to rest there. Traveller was buried outside the chapel. In a living tribute to the general, the college became Washington and Lee University.

TIMELINE

In the year . . .

1810   Robert moved to Alexandria, Virginia, with his family.
        Age 3

1813   his father, Henry Lee, left the family.

1825   he entered the U.S. Military Academy at West Point, New York.

1829   he graduated from West Point.
he was commissioned as a lieutenant in the U.S. Army Corps of Engineers.
his mother, Ann Carter Lee, died.
        Age 22

1831   he married Mary Custis.

1846   he was sent to fight in the Mexican-American War.
        Age 39

1855   he joined the cavalry in Texas.

1861   the American Civil War began.
he resigned from the U.S. Army and returned to Virginia.
he was put in charge of Virginia's military forces.
        Age 54

1862   he was put in command of the Confederate Army of Northern Virginia.
        Age 55

1863   he led the Confederates to victory at Chancellorsville, Virginia.
his army suffered a serious defeat at Gettysburg.

1865   he surrendered to Union general U. S. Grant at Appomattox Court House, Virginia.
Robert became president of Washington College in Lexington, Virginia.
        Age 58

1870   he died in Lexington, Virginia.
        Age 63

PRISONER OF WAR

When Robert E. Lee died, he was still officially a prisoner of war on release from prison. His U.S. citizenship had been taken away from him.

After the war, former Confederate leaders had to ask the U.S. government for a pardon. The pardon would excuse them for leading Southerners in a war against the Union. To get back their citizenship, the leaders also had to take an oath. They had to promise to remain loyal to the United States.

Lee would not take the oath at first. He wanted to make sure that the U.S. president, Andrew Johnson, would not treat Southerners badly. When he felt that Johnson's government would be fair to the South, he signed his oath. But the pardon he requested never came.

Lee's request was lost for one hundred years. In 1970, an office worker at the National Archives in Washington, D.C., found it among some other papers. Finally, in 1975, Lee's citizenship was restored by an act of Congress.

Congress meets at the U.S. capitol in Washington D.C.

FURTHER READING

Aller, Susan Bivin. *Ulysses S. Grant.* Minneapolis: Lerner Publications Company, 2005. Find out more about Lee's greatest Civil War foe.

Damon, Duane. *Growing Up in the Civil War 1861 to 1865.* Minneapolis: Lerner Publications Company, 2003. Primary-source material adds to the story of children working and fighting to defend their way of life during war.

Day, Nancy. *Your Travel Guide to Civil War America.* Minneapolis: Lerner Publications Company, 2001. This guide explores everyday life during the Civil War on farms, in cities, on battlefields, and in camp.

Murphy, Jim. *The Boy's War: Confederate and Union Soldiers Talk About the Civil War.* New York: Clarion Books, 1990. Diary entries, letters, and photographs describe the experiences of the Civil War's youngest soldiers.

Ransom, Candice. *Children of the Civil War.* Minneapolis: Carolrhoda Books, 1998. This book explores the lives of children caught in the conflict between the North and the South.

Ransom, Candice. *Willie McLean and the Civil War Surrender.* Minneapolis: Carolrhoda Books, 2005. This book tells the story of eleven-year-old Willie McLean and how he becomes a witness to Lee's surrender at Appomattox.

Schott, Jane A. *Abraham Lincoln.* Minneapolis: Lerner Publications Company, 2002. Read about the life of the man who fought to preserve the Union during the Civil War.

WEBSITES

AmericanCivilWar.com
http://www.americancivilwar.com
This comprehensive website features a timeline, battle details, maps, biographies, famous speeches, and photographs.

Arlington House, the Robert E. Lee Memorial
http://www.nps.gov/arho/index.htm
This website offers information on the history of Arlington House and how it became Arlington National Cemetery. It's "In Depth" section features biographies of the Lees and a virtual tour of the house.

Stratford Hall
http://www.stratfordhall.org
The Robert E. Lee Memorial Association website provides a history of the Lees of Virginia and their home. The site also features articles on slavery and plantation life.

SELECT BIBLIOGRAPHY

Davis, Burke. *Gray Fox: Robert E. Lee and the Civil War.* 1956. Reprint, with a new introduction by the author, Springfield, NJ: Burford Books, 1998.

Freeman, Douglas Southall. *Lee.* 1934. Reprint, New York: Scribner, 1997.

Nolan, Alan T. *Lee Considered: General Robert E. Lee and Civil War History.* Chapel Hill: University of North Carolina Press, 1991.

Walsh, George. *"Damage Them All You Can": Robert E. Lee's Army of Northern Virginia.* New York: Forge, 2002.

INDEX

Acknowledgments

The images in this book are used with the permission of: Library of Congress, pp. 4 (LC-DIG-cwpbh-03116), 11 (LC-USZ62-98811), 16 (LC-USZC2-2939), 17 (LC-USZC4-2851), 18 (LC-USZC4-528), 20 (LC-USZG2-8252), 22 (LC-USZC4-995), 24 (LC-USZC4-8104), 25 (LC-USZC2-2991), 30 (LC-USZ62-4373), 31 (LC-USZ62-21988), 34 (LC-USZC4-1866), 35 (LC-USZ62-103217), 36 (LC-USZ62-116520), 39 (LC-DIG-cwbp-03908), 40 (LC-DIG-cwpb-06234), 41 (LC-USZ62-11095); Courtesy of Cornell University Library, Making of America Digital Collection, *Harper's New Monthly Magazine*, vol. 76, issue 454 (March 1888), p. 7; Robert E. Lee Memorial Association, Stratford Hall Plantation, p. 9; © CORBIS, p. 10; U.S. Army Corps of Engineers, p. 12; Virginia State Library and Archives, pp. 15, 37, 42; National Archives, pp. 23, 32; Courtesy of Cornell University Library, Making of America Digital Collection, *The Century*, vol. 32, issue 4 (Aug. 1886), pp. 28, 29; West Point Museum Collection, United States Military Academy, p. 33; A. A. M. Van der Heyden/IPS, p. 45. Front cover: Library of Congress (LC-DIG-cwpb-04402). Back cover: Museum of the Confederacy, Richmond, Virginia, Photography by Katherine Wetzel. **For quoted material:** pp. 16, 29, 33, 43, Douglas Southall Freeman, *Lee* (1934; reprint, New York: Scribner, 1997); p. 30, J. Roderick Heller III and Carolyn Ayres Heller, eds., *The Confederacy Is on Her Way Up the Spout: Letters to South Carolina*, 1861–1864 (Athens: University of Georgia Press, 1992); p. 31, Mark Mayo Boatner III, *The Civil War Dictionary* (New York: David McKay Co., 1959).